I0365955

Credit goes to
author O'Ceanic,
and the team of designers,
photographers, cartoonists,
and editors at the publisher: D'Moon

first edition: 2025
Quote Art: see book "Math and Music"

ISBN: 978-1-933187-33-4

Slight variations may occur
as part of the print-on-demand process
since each book is manufactured in its entirety.

Your feedback is most welcome ~
publisher@worldculturepictorial.com

Oceanic

d'moon books

Words are to express as into cultures are born souls. Latin-alphabet English, and picture-composed Chinese, 2 out of top 3 most used languages (half of world can speak more than one), that has inspired book series

『random notes on road 游子远』-

《orNot知》 (2025)

《aFar 远》 (2024)

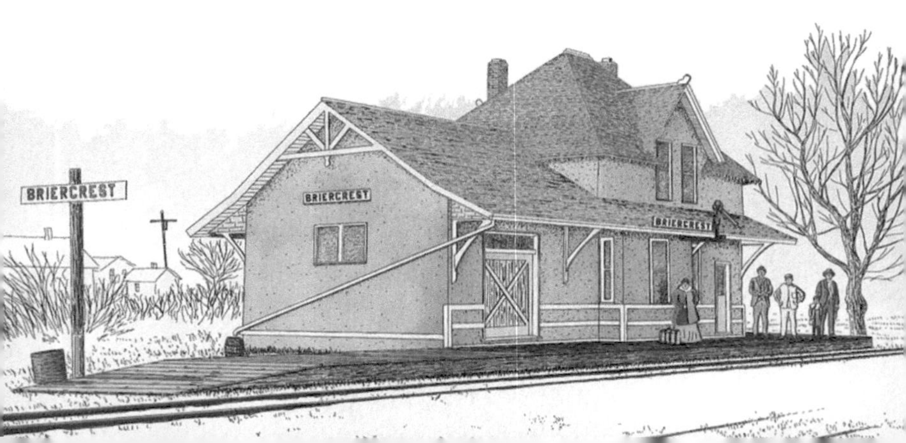

无论多遥远

吉祥

Latin-alphabet
and picture-words
are paired up,
no translation
but connections,
common notion
of Plato,
of LaoTsu, Confucius,
of da Vinci, Shakespeare,
of BaiJuyi, SuShi.
Broad content spans
over thousands of years.

无论在何方

...

The disembarked left.
Whistle blows.
Hop on!
All aboard!
Nature is unfolding more...

...

Train and book.
Notebook and pen.
See more. Read more.
A journey of learning.
A journey of growing wise.

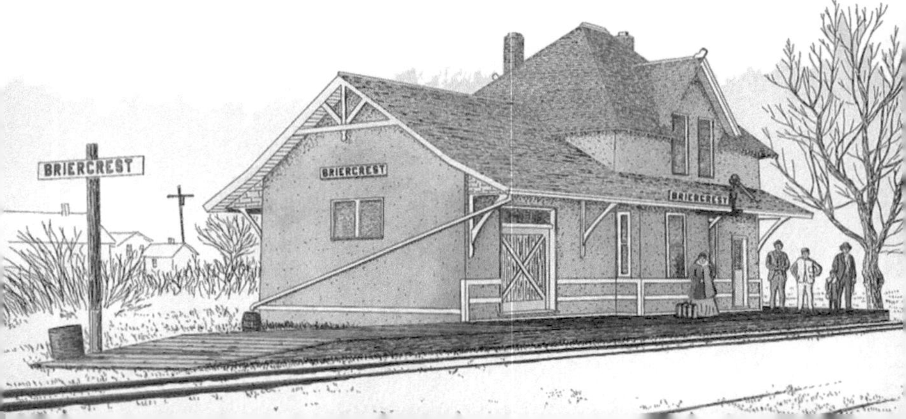

伴奏着火车永恒的节奏
大自然,山水林云,
无始无端,神秘奇妙.
植物万千,从娇艳的花儿到
暴风狂雨中百年屹立的苍
松,皆都仅仅依靠雨露阳光.
飞禽走兽大都"鸟为食亡".
世人,生为文化人,
好奇,愿解困惑,求知识...

望望火车窗外,大自然
源源无际,永恒广阔,知识
落满山山水水树木云端,
地大的书桌,
天大的书.
伴奏着火车永恒的节奏.

Good Luck!

∘ i ∘

mysterious (Einstein)
be content (LaoTsu)
lift veil (Percy Shelley)
self-knowledge (Lord Tennyson)
a corner of universe (Huxley)
never regret (da Vinci)
mirror (Bernard Shaw)
discover more (Plato)
self to copy (Goldsmith)
wisdom temple (Franklin)

吉祥安康

○ i ○

数不清.知不知,上.

1700多年的对联:只求半称心

熙熙攘攘与陋室铭

意大利宇航员太空颂信可乐

食素戒烟书房康熙:62年

天下父母同心.孔明《诫子书》

知人知己? 真挚友谊齐天

高速度时代,古训稳如泰山

Quote Art

◦ II ◦

math & music
silver crown
doctor: no clue
drizzle
hail to hero
a child's dream
don't go away
couch & ego
the dice

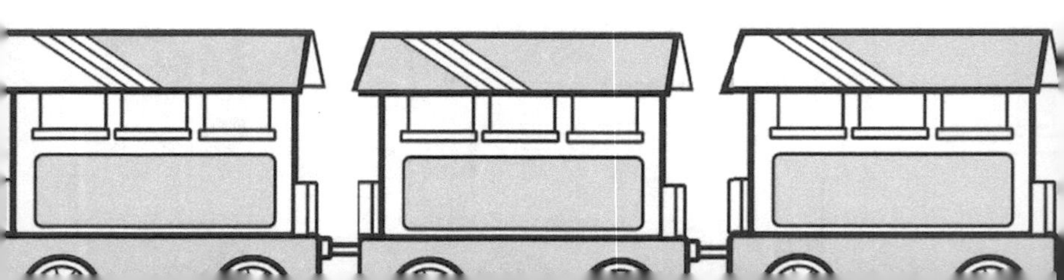

成语典故。慧言妙语

○ II ○

十步芳草　(卉土圭)
百步穿柳　(陌洎畾)
千叮万嘱　(早卓朝)
迟迟吾行　(五吾梧)
晨兢夕厉　(夕夙多)
高山流水　(石拓磊)
九曲十八弯(旮旯究)
路遥知马力
日久见人心

humor. wine. poetry

◦ iii ◦

greatest perfection
love not Man less
no more by thee
a friend to all
too much of anything
never wrestle with...
try to get even
fragile dew-drop
where I am going
out of the cloud-folds
we repeatedly do
habit, character

天高路远

◦ iii ◦

雨林古体诗首版

《我弹朝露》 4言诗
《痛失》 8言诗
《云水沉》 7言诗
《老子崂山》 7言诗
《五月》 7言诗
《瞬间》 8言诗
《雪花》 6言诗
《愿》 7言诗

The most
beautiful thing
we can experience is
the mysterious.
It is the source of
all true art and science.
~ Albert Einstein

The noblest pleasure
is the joy of understanding.

~ Leonardo da Vinci

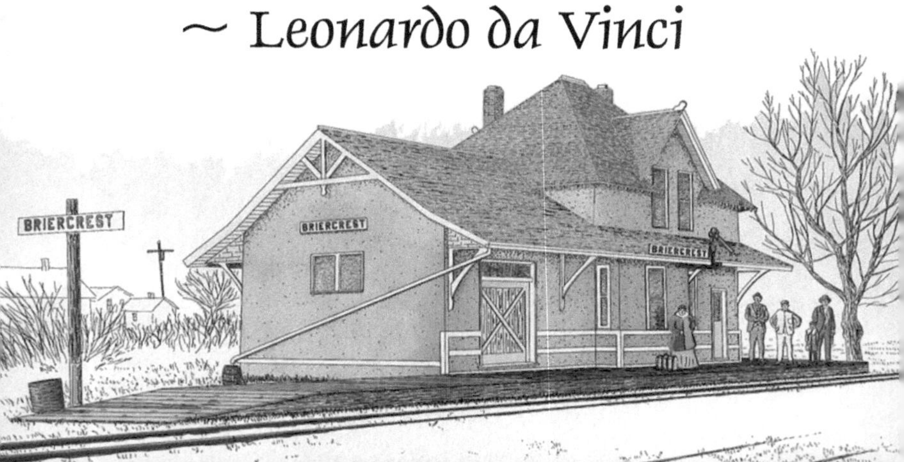

数不清.知不知,上.

宇宙浩瀚星星云游数不清.
天地间生灵数不清.
娃娃落地哇哇大哭:
是不情愿来到人世间?
还是喜庆独立?
无从得知.
芸芸众生貌相皆不同.
暗示不同的命运?
命难知难料,
即使借助西方的12星座,
东方的12宫.
知不知,上. (老子)

人生之舟云天雾罩朦朦胧胧...
孔夫子言: 学而不厌.
荀子劝学:
不积跬步, 无以致千里;
不积小流, 无以致江海.
「学」与「悟」起航扬帆.

Be content with what you have; rejoice in the way things are. When you realize there is nothing lacking, the whole world belongs to you.

~ LaoTsu

The greatest wealth is to live content with little.

~ Plato

1700多年对联:只求半称心

灵隐寺对联挂了1700年,
"人生哪能多如意
万事只求半称心".
智慧. 14个字开释了苏轼的
"问汝平生功业,
黄州惠州儋州."
无论生活何等曲折流离颠沛,
大诗人"矢志不渝" -
苏东坡始终是苏东坡!
难以言喻的艰辛, 何以称心?
"境随心转". 苏东坡开荒种地,
采野果酿酒,与农夫渔父和尚
开怀畅谈...
千百年来栩栩如生.

Poetry lifts the
veil from the
hidden beauty of the
world, and makes
familiar objects be
as if they were
not familiar.

~ Percy Bysshe Shelley

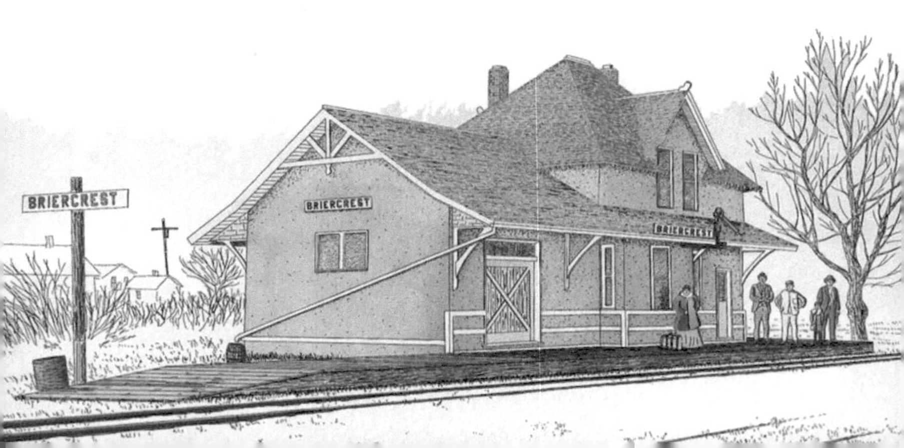

熙熙攘攘与陋室铭

司马迁《史记》语:
"天下熙熙,皆为利来;
天下攘攘,皆为利往".

也有往来陋室,
"谈笑有鸿儒"(刘禹锡):
"山不在高,有仙则名.
水不在深,有龙则灵.
斯是陋室,惟吾德馨.
苔痕上阶绿,草色入帘青.
谈笑有鸿儒,往来无白丁.
可以调素琴,阅金经.
无丝竹之乱耳,无案牍之劳形."

熙熙攘攘,忙忙碌碌.
调素琴阅金经谈笑风声.
大千世界,
志不同,
道不同...

Self-reverence,
self-knowledge,
self-control;
these three alone
lead life to
sovereign power.
~ Alfred Lord Tennyson

意大利宇航员太空颂信可乐

何等缘分!
意大利女宇航员返程之前
用中文古词把书法家王曦之
353年4月(距今已1667年)对大自
然的赞叹送上天空:“仰观宇宙之
大,俯察品类之盛,所以游目骋怀,
足以极视听之娱,信可乐也”.

缘,牵线搭桥世人相知相识.
超越难以想象1600年的距离,
超越文化文字各异的距离.
夜晚天空奥妙深沉,
星星眨眨眼推推搡搡,
隐隐约约闪现出三个字:
何为缘?

✦orNot✦random notes on road

(continued from >)

Two days before she landed on Earth, the beauty of space and Chinese literature resonated on her Twitter account. The text she quoted is from Orchid Pavilion, by Chinese calligrapher Wang Xizhi (303-361). Before long, her posts went viral on Twitter with thousands of retweets, likes and replies.

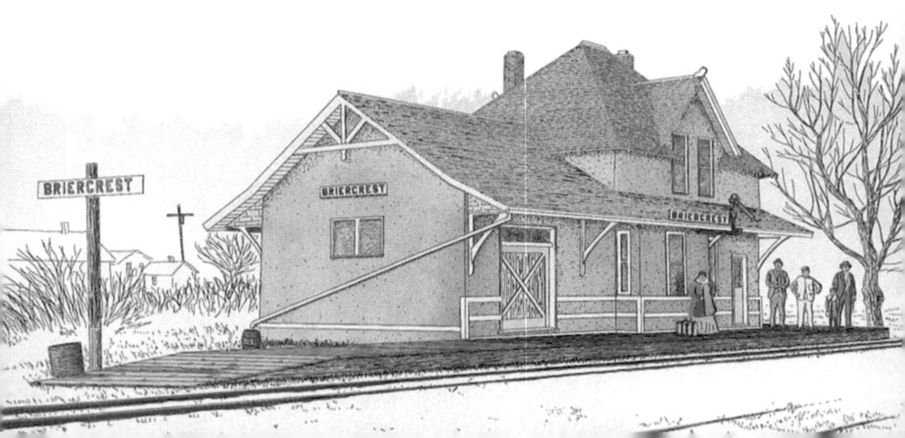

Oct'22, in space, Samantha Cristoforetti, the 1st Italian female astronaut posted several lines of a famous ancient Chinese poem on Twitter to share her joy. "Looking up, I see the immensity of the cosmos; bowing my head, I look at the multitude of the world. The gaze flies, the heart expands, the joy of the senses can reach its peak, and indeed, this is true happiness," it said.

(<—continued)

There is only one corner
of the universe you can
be certain of improving,
and that's
your own self.
~ Aldous Huxley

Some ships are
wooden ships, but those
ships may sink. The
best ships are friendships, and
to those ships, we drink.
~ Irish Proverb

食素戒烟书房.康熙:62年

3位在位时间最长的皇帝-
第一: 康熙帝,61年318天
第二: 乾隆帝,60年
第三: 汉武帝刘彻,54年
2位戒烟:康熙帝,乾隆帝
1位偏爱食素:康熙帝

食素.戒烟.书房.
康熙化解了宫廷的山珍海味,
抽烟的诱惑,离别前仍然伏案
畅春园清溪书屋...仿佛白居易
诗句的情景...[负冬日]:
杲杲冬日出, 照我屋南隅.
负暄闭目坐, 和气生肌肤.
白居易[闲居]:
绵袍拥两膝, 竹几支双臂.
心足即为富...何必居高位.
(*在位时间最长的皇帝*)

Learning is the only thing
the mind never exhausts,
never fears, and
never regrets.

~ da Vinci

Common sense is
not so common.

~ Voltaire

I live in that solitude which
is painful in youth, but
delicious in the years of
maturity.

~ Einstein

天下父母同心.《诫子书》

普天下父母都爱孩子.
盼望孩子成才,成才之道
正如智慧的诸葛亮在
《诫子书》指明:
非淡泊无以明志,
非宁静无以致远.夫君子之行,
静以修身,俭以养德,
夫学需静也,才需学也,
非学无以广才,非志无以成学.

如今物质令人眼花缭乱,
百万富翁林立.何以引导挂着
金钥匙的沿着孔明的淡泊
明志宁静致远之道成大器?
天下父母同心.
难题各异.
难.

You use
a glass mirror
to see your face;
you use
works of art
to see your soul.
~ George Bernard Shaw

You can discover more
about a person in an hour
of play than in a year of
conversation.
~ Plato

知人知己?真挚友谊齐天

周围是陌生人,无识不知.
熟人亲戚,认识,知面,知心?
知人者智,自知者明.(老子)
明智者,或许多些喜剧.
幸运者,有平生心迹最相亲(白居易)
同类相从,同声相应. 李白:
行来北凉岁月深, 感君贵义轻黄金
苏轼: 知君仙骨无寒暑
知音好友谈笑诗如画 –
李白《戏赠杜甫》
饭颗山头逢杜甫,顶戴笠子日卓午.
借问别来太瘦生,总为从前作诗苦.
听到李商隐哭师友的悲痛?
平生风义兼师友,不敢同君哭寝门.

挚友间情谊心声如同蓝天的云,
风中落雨,冬日雪花飘飘洒洒...
问半月问圆月:
何时聚首畅谈?

People seldom improve when
they have
no other model
but themselves to copy.

~ Oliver Goldsmith

The more the soul is filled
with wisdom, the less it
desires petty gains.

~ Plato

The doorstep to the temple of
wisdom is
a knowledge of
our own ignorance.

~ Benjamin Franklin

时代高速度,古训稳如泰山

高科技高速度,时代变迁.
然而天地间的人始终是文化人
普天下赞赏诚信;
赞赏礼之用.和为贵.(孔子)
由语言而文字而书法艺术,
几千年来陪伴着学童成长,
陪伴着成长了的学童走天涯,
普天下欣赏那坐如钟走如风
静如松的自信.
相信自己.
志不在年少,志不在年高.
生命是奇迹,太极是哲理.
从云手,气沉丹田,沉肩坠肘开始
去僵取灵活,去浮而沉稳,坦然清
醒而四两拨千斤:自强自立,和.

山岳巍然屹立江河奔流.古往今
来哲理智慧依然稳稳开悟人生;
现代节奏高速度...

QUOTE "Math & Music"
to introduce the poem

Numbers
are sketched
into tones
Equations
stretched into tunes
I'm fond of faithful math
I hear my heart
humming
lyrical poems

✦知否✦游子运

火车不紧不慢,
时不时鸣叫地前进.
车窗外
风吹树动,
风止叶静,
恰如
文武之道
“一张一驰”.

高科技, 高速度,
如同车窗外近处的
景物飞快闪过.
不仅不赏心悦目,
且令人头晕目眩。

QUOTE "SILVER CROWN" to introduce the poem

The sunlight has dyed
my hair golden brown,
Shone upon my way
all years round...
A poetic soul is ever young,
ever young.
Though soon the snow, the moon
is to give me a silver crown.

人心， 深而沉，
奥妙的大自然祥和平静，
也给予了世人祥和平静，
像远处的星空
缓缓地静中行，
以养怡心神…
对窗外凝视了一阵，
视线转回，合上了
笔记本…

QUOTE "CHEMISTRY OF JEALOUSY" to introduce the poem

A doctor
  beyond a doctor
Concentrates
  over half a century...
On one deadly symptom
A lethal virus,
  not uncommon -
Chemistry of
  Jealousy

十　　十年寒窗
草　　十步芳草
卉　　百卉含英
土　　土生土长
桂　　桂子飘香
涯　　天涯知己

QUOTE "ME AND DRIZZLE"
to introduce the poem

泊　　澹泊以明志

　　宁静以致远

柏　　岁寒松柏

白　　白头相守

皛　　天皛无云

百　　百步穿柳

陌　　八街九陌

QUOTE "CATASTROPHE SHOCKED" to introduce the poem

– Hail to Hero

urricane Katrina rages,
blows in thirty feet high flood,
burying town by town
but home's roof.
Catastrophe must be shocked
by a stark contrast

千　　千叮万嘱
阡　　阡陌纵横
什　　什伍东西
早　　早出暮归
卓　　卓育菁莪
朝　　朝不虑夕

QUOTE "MET THE WISEST" to introduce the poem

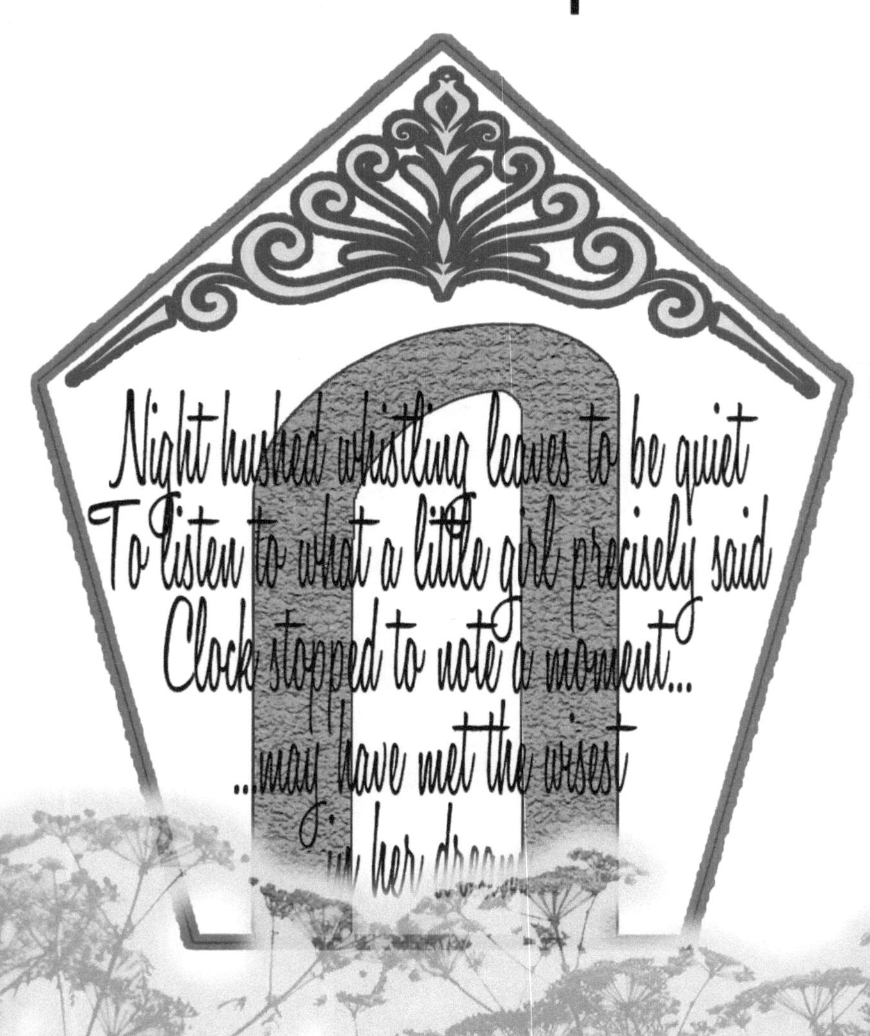

五　　五十步
　　　　笑百步
伍　　参参伍伍
吾　　迟迟吾行
梧　　梧风之鸣
寤　　夙夜梦寤
悟　　恍然大悟

QUOTE "DON'T GO AWAY" to introduce the poem

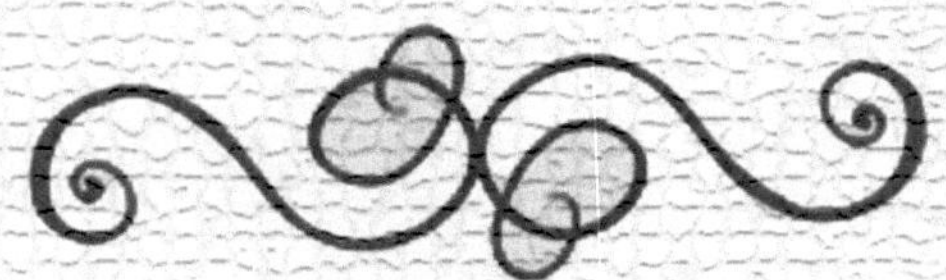

I'll see you no more,
though I've never
seen you before.
You left Life. . . "How so?"
Pain lingers on shore.
Eyes sore.

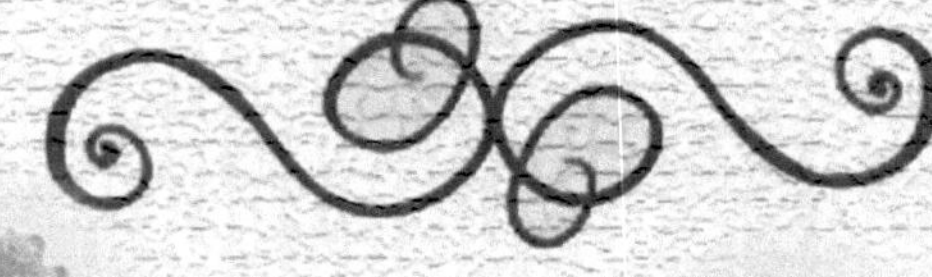

夕　　晨兢夕厉

外　　超然物外

名　　实至名归

岁　　岁月如流

多　　多多少少

夙　　夜寝夙兴

QUOTE "Couch Magician" to introduce the poem

Do you believe
Couch is
a magician,
at the center of Luxury,
chubby, solidly heavy,
to spare muscle's energy,
relieve intensity,
to feed the desire
for Ego,
soothe anxiety?

山　　高山流水
岩　　岩栖谷饮
石　　人非木石
蹉　　日月蹉跎
跎　　秤不离砣
磊　　磊磊落落

QUOTE "FATE ROLLS THE DICE ii" to introduce the poem

Fate bestows
the child a fortune,
when Wealth is a curse
Knowledge pollutes...
Is it possible
when Fate rolls the dice
(if not for all of us)
we deliver our [illegible] move?

九　　九曲十八弯
旮　　旮旮旯旯
旯　　山旮旯儿
究　　研精究微
九鼎不足为重
路遥知马力
日久见人心

✦orNot✦random notes on road

Wine is one of the most civilized... most natural things brought to the greatest perfection... offers a greater... appreciation...

~ Ernest Hemingway

The sun is warm, the sky is clear, The waves are dancing fast and bright, Blue isles and snowy mountains wear The purple noon's transparent might...

~ Percy Bysshe Shelley

列车铿锵有力地前进，乌云密布的天空渐渐地远去了.窗外是平原，山林.好个"白云白云深处有人家"(杜牧)：青青草地,牛羊成群,悠哉悠哉...带回了嘻戏童年的记忆,更带回了亲朋挚友的嘱托...

古往今来,无计其数的人踏上了远程,能有多少返回家园团聚?别离之际又几人没有忘却王维的劝：

劝君更尽一杯酒，
西出阳关无故人。

There is pleasure in the
pathless woods,
there is rapture in the
lonely shore,
there is society where none
intrudes, by the deep sea,
and music in its roar;
I love not Man the less,
but Nature more.

~ Lord Byron

雨林✦四言诗

《我弹朝露》

一山浓雾
绿水一湖
白鹅漫步
我弹朝露
春落枝头
借梅问路

No more
by thee
my steps shall be,
For ever and
for ever.
~ Alfred Lord Tennyson

And ask ye
why these
sad tears stream?
~ Alfred Lord Tennyson

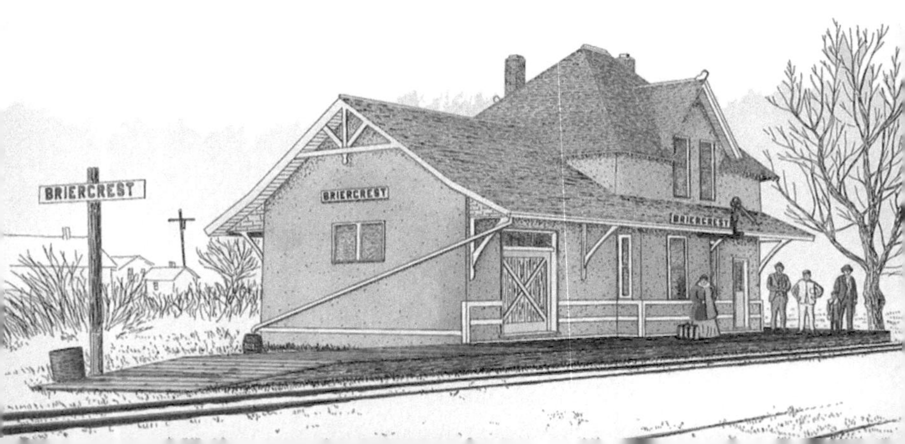

雨林✦八言诗

《痛失》

噩耗惊魂泪涌如泉
闭关掩面雷雨连天
三十年思念别无言
松枝簇笑颜梦里谈

A friend
to all is
a friend
to none.

~ Aristotle

Words are easy,
like the wind;
faithful friends are
hard to find.

~ William Shakespeare

雨林✦七言诗

《云水沉》

风起雨落云水沉
伞下湖边念故人
相识相知皆天运
地杰育就仙骨魂

Too much of
anything is
bad, but
too much
Champagne is
just right.

~ Mark Twain

A man cannot make him
laugh—but that's
no marvel; he
drinks no wine.

~ Shakespeare

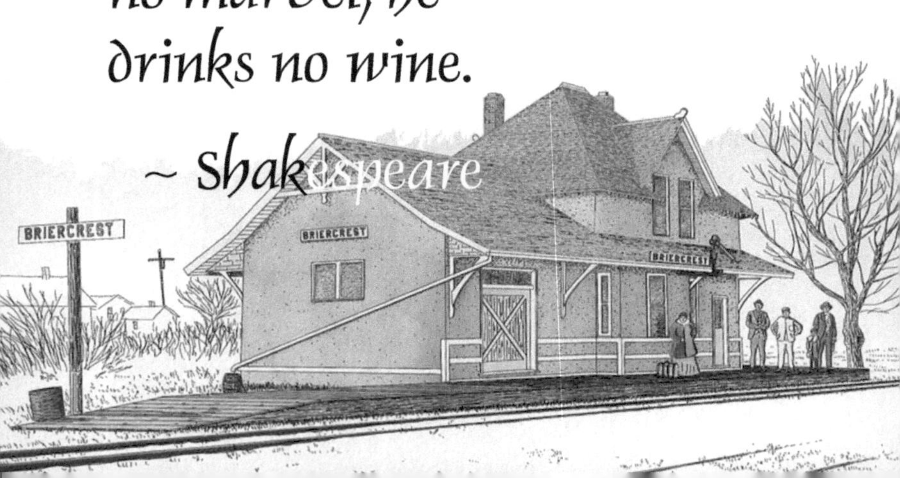

雨林✦七言诗

《老子崂山》

仙鹤腾空祥中翔
风云变幻道无常
崂山泉水清又亮
千古酿酒醉魂香

'Animals are my friends...' 'I learned long ago, never to wrestle with a pig. You get dirty, and besides, the pig likes it. '

~ George Bernard Shaw

When my cats aren't happy, I'm not happy. Not because I care about their mood but because I know they're just sitting there thinking up ways to get even.

~ Percy Bysshe Shelley

雨林✦七言诗

《五月》

五月间半红半绿
好似秋枫邻松树
仰望高空天颔首
欲语不言抚万物

Give
sorrow words; the
grief that does not speak
knits up the o-er
wrought heart and
bids it break.

~ William Shakespeare

... but a day;
A fragile dew-drop on its
perilous way
From a tree's summit.

~ John Keats

雨林✦八言诗

《瞬间》

风华英年一枝独蔫
挚友苦劝近者断言
瞬间，　瞬间
至诚至善宇天行健
星闪星灭大地遮面
瞬间，　瞬间

I don't know
where I am going,
but I am on my way.
~ Voltaire

Out of the bosom of the Air,
Out of the cloud-folds of
her garments shaken,
Over the woodlands brown
and bare,
Over the harvest-fields
forsaken,
Silent, and soft, and slow
Descends the snow.

~ Henry Wadsworth
Longfellow

BRIERCREST
BRIERCREST
BRIERCREST

雨林✦六言诗

《雪花》

夜降雪花起舞
灯闪漫漫银树
宁静中轻移步
白茫茫隐归路

We are
what we repeatedly do.
Excellence, then, is
not an act, but a habit.
~ Aristotle

Character is simply
habit long continued.
~ Plato

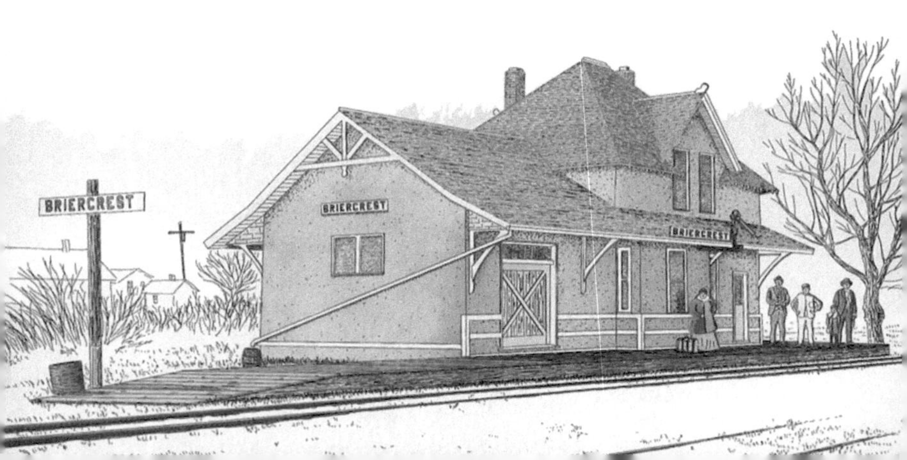

雨林✦七言诗

《愿》

人心古朴‘外星客’?
我行我素笑呵呵;
人有心愿天有情,
恶风浪中信天翁。

www.ingramcontent.com/pod-product-compliance
Lightning Source LLC
Chambersburg PA
CBHW060540080526
44586CB00012B/802

* 9 7 8 1 9 3 3 1 8 7 3 3 4 *